20 Minutes to Live

20 Minutes to Live

Discovering Miracles, Perseverance, and the Power of Prayer

Kathryn M. Pistoresi

Copyright © 2023
Kathryn M. Pistoresi

Performance Publishing
McKinney, TX

All Worldwide Rights Reserved.

All rights reserved. No part of this publication may be reproduced, stored in a retrieval system or transmitted, in any form or by any means, electronic, mechanical, recorded, photocopied, or otherwise, without the prior written permission of the copyright owner, except by a reviewer who may quote brief passages in a review.

ISBN: 978-1-961781-18-4

I dedicate this book to…

To my family…

To my "Angels"…

To Dr. Nick Hansa…

To Dr. Bob Laughlin…

To my husband…I love you more!

To God be the Glory!

Shelley's Testimonial

God is good... God is great... God is full of grace... so is Kathy.

Kathy's story is one of abundant blessings, inspiration, faith, and ultimately a fierce determination to live life... really live life... embracing every day with a joyful and thankful heart... the way God intended her to live it.

Kathy was on overdrive for years, as a wife, mother, daughter, fitness therapist, nutritional consultant, friend, sister, and grandma. She was very driven to succeed in everything she did – 110%. She loves the Lord with all her heart. He has gotten her through many, many personal and professional challenges, as well as health and medical problems. She thrived on stress: the more challenges the better... that is... until she crashed... big time!

Kathy was diagnosed with ARDS (acute respiratory distress syndrome) on February 2, 2012. She was placed in a medically induced coma and on a respirator twice, and was ultimately in the hospital for sixty-five days. She became septic, had total system failure, and was not expected to live. She had seven toes amputated as a result of a powerful medication given to her to save her life. She had deadly blood clots that threatened her life. She had a G-tube inserted in her stomach as she could not eat. She ultimately had a tracheostomy as she could not breathe on her own. She was also blessed by God each and every second of each and every day!

Kathy dreamed of God, and she talked to Him in her mind. He healed her. She was given another chance at life – one she does not take lightly. She lives each and every day like it is her last. She is thankful each and every day and shows all of us the love of Jesus by the way she loves the Lord. Her eyes shine bright with the love of Jesus and her smile lights up a room. Everyone gravitates to her. She is the work of the Lord: she is alive, stronger than ever, loving her precious husband, her family, her friends, and most of all, God. Kathy is full of God's grace! God blessed her with another chance at living her life and has blessed us with Kathy.

God is good... God is great... God is full of grace... so is Kathy.

Kathy had two secret weapons... Jesus Christ and Ken Pistoresi, her husband. The two of them never ever left her side. They were both there, holding her hand, loving her, and they still are!

Love,
Shelley Northrop
MSN, RN, PHN, Health Services Administrator for Kern County Superintendent of Schools

Our Family

Hi, I'm sure as you read my book, you will wonder who the characters are. I'm Kathy. I am married to Ken, and together we have five children. We are a blended family and have been married for over twenty-seven years.

My firstborn child is Chad, who is married to Hiedi. They have two children, Jagger and Brinkley. Chad sat by my bedside daily, ate his broccoli and chicken, and kept everyone believing I would be OK. Matthew was second born and is married to Tiffany. They have two children, Pierce and Carson. Matthew and Tiffany stayed by my side and played music he thought I would love. Amber is my third-born child. She and her husband, Nathan, have two children, Ethan and Ryann. Amber kept a journal throughout my hospitalization. Her journal helped me write this book.

Ken's eldest, Kristen, is married to Seth, and together they have six children: Audrey, Andrew, Lucas, Maddy, Jack, and Holly. Kristen helped so much with babysitting Amber's children so she could be at the hospital with me. Ken's second daughter, Katie, made sure that Ken had food when he came home to eat and shower and took really good care of our home and pets.

My three siblings also came to my rescue. Monte and his wife, Marilyn, live in Houston, TX. Their church and friends prayed for my healing. When I started my ketamine infusions, they came to California to take care of me. Becci and her husband, Tom, live in Johns Island, SC. They supported us, prayed for us, and called to check on me every day. Becci started a GoFundMe page that was circulated to all our friends in other states. Eric is married to Laura, and they live in Dallas, TX. They supported us in every way. Their church group and friends prayed. Eric set up a Bakersfield Memorial Hospital "Caring Bridge," where family members could share information about me and my progress. Anyone could go read the updates. He also came to help take care of me when I first arrived home. When I started my ketamine infusions, he came to California and took care of me for a week.

Our Angels

My angels are girlfriends and their husbands who put their lives on hold for us! Shelley, a registered nurse and administrator for the school districts in Kern County for thirty years, became our lead angel. She is a true leader! She made sure to ask the doctors and nurses the right questions at the right times. Shelley monitored my vitals and gave my family all the necessary explanations of what was going on at any given moment. She loved and encouraged my family every step of the way. She is married to Bill, and they have three children. Bill was at the hospital often and prayed over us and the kids. When I woke up, he would gently hold my hand and wipe my face after my coughing spells. To this day, he still holds my hand and asks if I'm OK. They have been part of our small group for fifteen years.

Lori and her husband, Les, have led our amazing small group for twenty years. Lori is a stay-at-home mom and supports Les in all his ministries throughout the USA. They have three children. She is a giver from start to finish! Les is a strong leader of couples and Men's Ministry. Together, they are very good at gathering people and helping them grow in their faith. Lori sat by my side, prayed for me, read to me, and made sure to help in any way she could. Les gathered hundreds of people to pray for us and held prayer vigils in the parking lot of the hospital.

Sandy and her husband Duane were among the first couples we met in Les and Lori's small group many years ago. Sandy is a stay-at-home mom, soft-spoken, and full of wisdom and grace. She would read to me, help bathe me or turn me, pray over me, or just sit and talk to me. Duane kept Ken encouraged and laughing.

Toni and her husband Greg were among the first six couples we met in that small group. They have four children, and Toni is a stay-at-home mom. Toni is quiet and serves the Lord in all that she does. She is crafty and unique in her giving. She read to me and did anything that was asked of her. Toni stayed by my side, praying over me and encouraging everyone around. Greg loves investing his time and energy in men's ministries of all kinds. Greg kept Ken encouraged through texts and phone calls.

Nancy and her husband, Dave, invited us to this small group many years ago. They have two children. Both were working full time when I got sick; however, when the need arose for another angel, Nancy made time to sit with me. She read to me and was the one rubbing my back when I went into anaphylactic shock. They encouraged and cared for us from the first time we joined the small group.

Through my sixty-five days in the hospital, many "angels" helped Ken and our kids in any way they could. We are grateful for every one of them! God provided everything we needed to survive this journey. Now, eleven years later, He still provides "angels" for support, encouragement, prayer, and rides to USC. God has multiplied the number of friends a thousand-fold!

As you can see, we have very special friends!

Contents

Life Changes in an Instant 1
Angels Sent from Heaven 5
Amber's Journal #1 7
Christ's Love 11
Amber's Journal #2 14
Pleas for Help 16
Amber's Journal #3 18
Out of the Coma and into the Light 21
Leaving ICU 25
Hail Mary 27
Meeting Jesus 30
Ken's Letter to Angels 32
I am Alive! 35
Leaving the Hospital 39
HealthSouth Rehabilitation Center 41
To God Be the Glory! 47
Be Still and Know that I Am God 49
Be Strong and Courageous 51
Mount Up with Wings Like Eagles 54
Ken's Precious Words 57
Blessings from God 58
Our Community Gathers 60
The Love of Grandkids 62
Frustration Arises 63
My First Speaking Engagement 64
Back to Rehabilitation 66

My Birthday..69
One Year After ARDS 71
Dependent on Drugs...73
New Opportunities at USC..76
My Ketamine Journey 81
What Have I Learned from the Last Eleven Years?........................85
Prayer Works...88

CHAPTER 1

Life Changes in an Instant

February 2, 2012
Ken

"Stay there, babe. I will come around and help you out of the car."

We walked slowly into the emergency room at Bakersfield Memorial Hospital. As we scanned the waiting room, we could see that there was only one chair left. The look on your face said it all! The guard on duty must have seen the fear in your eyes. He came over and immediately sat you down and called a nurse. Two minutes later, a nurse took your vitals and rushed us back to a gurney.

Your blood pressure was 50/30! Everyone was asking us questions. "How long has she been this way?" "What kind of meds is she on?" "What is she allergic to?"

There was a sense of urgency – we had to get you on a gurney and get help. Four nurses came in to work on you. They inserted an IV in your arm and put you on oxygen. Then came more questions. "Is she on any meds for her breathing?" "Has she seen a doctor recently?" "Who is her doctor?" I answered every question as best I could. As soon as they started the breathing treatment, you passed out!

We made it, I thought to myself. We are going to be here for three or four hours, you are going to feel better soon, and then we will go home. Then Dr. Aggarwal (the cardiologist on call) came in.

"I am so happy that you got her here when you did. If you had waited another hour, it would not have been a favorable outcome! We need to take her to the ICU, but we will have to wait for a bed to become available."

I was in shock! The emergency room was extremely busy. All I could hear were the heart monitors beeping, bells going off to alert the nurses, thoughts whirling around in my head, and you gasping for air. I thought you would die!

One of the nurses came back a little while later and said, "We're going to turn off the lights and let her rest." Compared to what was going on for the last hour or so, this felt like dead silence. With the lights out, I just sat there on the cold tile floor, still in shock.

An awful feeling came over me, not knowing what to do next. I asked myself, *what is the right thing to do now?* I realized I had no control over the situation and started to pray for God to save you.

Audibly, I heard God say, "How can you lose what is not yours? If I choose to take her home, will you still love Me?"

I was in a state of disbelief. I could not comprehend it! I did not have an answer! I could not say anything! *I am not OK with it!*

I was arguing with myself, and I realized He was stroking the back of my head with His hand. He asked me, "Will you still love Me if I take Kathy home? I love you."

In that moment, I surrendered! I gave up and opened my hands to him. I just melted in a puddle of tears, and at the same time I felt so much reassurance and so much peace. I still had a tremendous amount of fear, but right then, I knew that no matter what happened, I would be OK. I knew it would be devastating to lose you, but I knew that your fate was in God's hands.

I honestly thought, *OK, we are going to be here three or four days a week.* Then in the middle of the night, they transferred you to ICU. I called everyone in our family, friends, and Pastor Eric. We needed prayers!

Shortly thereafter, Dr. Aggarwal diagnosed you with acute respiratory distress syndrome (ARDS). This occurs when fluid builds up in the tiny elastic air sacs in your lungs. The fluid keeps your lungs from filling with enough air, meaning less oxygen reaches your bloodstream. Organs are deprived of the oxygen they require. ARDS typically occurs in people who are already critically ill, have significant injuries to their chest, or who are septic. In your case, asthma, double pneumonia, and sepsis brought you to this point.

Many individuals who develop ARDS do not survive! The risk of death increases with age and severity of illness. Individuals who survive ARDS can experience lasting damage to their lungs and patients end up being paraplegics or quadriplegics due to the lack of oxygen traveling to their limbs.

Let us go back to the beginning of our story.... How all this started.

On Friday, January 27, 2012, you woke up wheezing. I suggested that you call Dr. Hansa (our pulmonologist) and let him know what was going on. We were committed to helping our friends Pops and Sandy cater a wedding in Santa Barbara the next day. You called Dr. Hansa's office, and they gave you an antibiotic and an inhaler. You seemed surprisingly good Saturday morning, so we went ahead and drove to Santa Barbara.

Catering a wedding is a ton of work and fun! We were at a beautiful home on the beach, with a sloping yard up to the house. There was a massive staircase leading up to the veranda where we were serving champagne and appetizers. You must have run up and down those stairs fifty times that day. After we served dinner, I noticed you started coughing more and you seemed very tired. I told you to go to the truck and warm up while I finished cleaning up.

I finished working forty-five minutes later. You were coughing and you looked terrible. We drove to the hotel and stayed the night, hoping and praying you would be better in the morning. When we woke, you seemed better than the previous day. You really wanted to go to the beach to just sit for an hour and relax. After that, we drove back to our home in Bakersfield and talked about calling the doctor first thing Monday morning.

On Monday morning, you were worse. We called Dr Hansa's office, but he was not at work, so they told us to go to urgent care. I drove you to the nearest urgent care facility, where we ended up staying four and a half hours. You needed multiple breathing treatments, x-rays, and drugs. The doctor told you that you had the beginnings of pneumonia. You needed to see your pulmonologist the next day.

On Tuesday, I took you to see Dr. Hansa. He confirmed that you had pneumonia and put you on a different antibiotic. He also instructed you to perform breathing treatments every two hours. But on Wednesday, despite everything, you were worse.

For four days, you were sitting on the couch doing breathing exercises, because you could not breathe while lying down. I was worried sick! Then on Thursday, you were worse! I tried calling you three times during the day, but you did not answer. I finally got a hold of you at 4:30 PM. You were noticeably short with me and hung up on me. You did not sound like yourself, and you had never hung up on me before. I told you I was coming home to pick you up and take you to the hospital. When I arrived home to pick you up, you looked horrible! Little did we know your battle was only just beginning.

CHAPTER 2

Angels Sent from Heaven

Ken

Dear Kathy,

We have the most amazing community of friends! We call them angels. They have been here since day one, praying, sending messages, and spreading the word that you are deathly ill!

Within the first few days, Les, leader of our Bible study group, called to tell me that he and other friends would be in the parking lot across the street from the hospital, praying for you that night. He asked if I or anyone else in the family would like to come over and join him. I asked Amber (our daughter) if she would like to go, since we were the only two in your room that evening. She said yes.

I must tell you how overwhelming it was to see all these friends standing in the parking lot, shining their phones towards your room, praying for us! We needed this support so badly! We were both overwhelmed by the outpouring of love, hugs, and prayers. Our hearts were full of emotion and gratitude. It has been an exhausting week!

Everyone prayed for your healing and God's perfect WILL. This prayer vigil was just the perfect reminder of God's love for us. He has provided us with amazing friends, whom we can do life with on a deep, nurturing level.

This was a first for Amber. So many friends embraced her. Prayed for her and you. These amazing friends of ours, whom we have spent many hours with over the last twenty years, are now praying for us through each day.

Thank You, Lord, for giving us this beautiful community.

CHAPTER 3

Amber's Journal #1

Wednesday, February 8, 2012
Amber

Dear Mom, you have been hospitalized for six days in ICU. The first four days, you were breathing from an oxygen mask; you had a morphine drip, an anti-anxiety medication, and antibiotics. You have multiple organ failures (heart, lungs, kidneys). Your oxygen level is consistently below 90. The hospital says they have done all they can do. Dr. Hansa encouraged us to limit our talking, because every time you wanted to speak, you would remove your mask. Then your oxygen level would drop below ninety, which was not a good thing.

You are in an extreme amount of pain. The nurse asked you your pain level and you said nine out of ten. At your best, you said six out of ten.

Your friends all want to see you. The first couple of days here, Ken, Chad, Matt, Tiffany, me, Shelley, Bill, Lori, Les, Toni, Greg, Pastor Eric, all came to see you.

After day two, we decided to cut off visitors to only immediate family. You have an enormous number of friends who love you! You wanted to try to talk to everyone when they came in, but you could barely breathe. You were not improving!

I did explain to your friends that as much as I am sure you would love to see them and have their support; you just needed to relax and heal. Everyone understood. The only friend we have allowed in is Shelley. For one, she is a nurse. She knows how to explain things to us in lay terms. She is comforting, encouraging, and I trust that she knows what she is talking about. She has really been amazing.

Chad stays calm and reassuring that you will be OK. Sunday, you were stable, and we were all here with you all day. I left the hospital Sunday night around 7:00 PM. "Go home and spend time with Ethan, Ryann, and Nate. I will start getting better tomorrow."

I said, "I love you."

You said, "I love you!"

Obviously, I was still incredibly nervous and did not sleep all night. On Monday morning, I woke up to a text message saying that the doctor just came in and they were going to ventilate you right away. I knew this was the only way that you were going to be able to heal, but I was scared just knowing you would be on the ventilator. You not being able to respond and interact with us was a challenging thing to grasp. But if this is how you would heal and breathe, then that is what needed to happen.

All day Monday, I watched you breathe easier. You had less pain in your chest. The doctor started you at 100% oxygen and by midday Monday, it was down to 80%. On Tuesday, you were down to 60% oxygen. This was a significant improvement. The nurse and respiratory therapist were impressed with how well you responded so quickly. They said you are such a healthy woman and how important it is that you have taken care of yourself. Your health is on your side, Mom.

All day Tuesday was smooth; you were resting and getting what you needed. This morning Dr. Hansa came in and said you were doing well. He lowered your oxygen to 50%, also a slight improvement.

So, if today goes well, tomorrow you could ease up on the paralytic. We will take any small increments of good news we can get! Diane also brought by a huge care basket for Chad, Matt, Ken, and me, with magazines, snacks, water, toothbrushes, floss, candy (for Ken), a blanket and pillow, and crossword puzzles.

I am enjoying the blanket and pillow. They keep it freezing here. Nurses come in and turn you around every two hours. They also clean your mouth out and moisturize your lips. All the nurse's comment on your great nails, hands, teeth, skin (you still have great skin and you have been in ICU for six days). I am blessed to have such a pretty mama!

Ken says when he stays here with you all night, he whispers in your ear how much he is enjoying his milk and cookies! Ha! That is Ken – he always has a way of making light of the situation.

I have been talking with Uncle Eric, Uncle Monte and Marilyn, and Aunt Becci every day. They have started prayer chains for you.

Uncle Eric started a Bakersfield Memorial Hospital (Caring Bridge) website for us to update our status throughout the day. I put a pretty picture of you on the site. Chad and I have been updating it.

Matt just went back to work today, but he will be coming to the hospital when he gets off around 5:00 PM. He has been off work since last Friday. He wanted to be here with you all the time. You are stable right now, so he went to work today. Chad goes back and forth between work and here throughout the day. Ken just brought me a sandwich, so we sat there and talked for an hour. The nurse started you on a small amount of nutrition. "Your mom may or may not be able to tolerate it," she said.

You are maintaining well with a small amount of nutrition. Oxygen is still at 50%. You are still on regular doses of anti-anxiety medication. Shelley stopped in for an hour to check on you. Chad, Shelley, and I looked at your x-rays. Your nurse Jodi has been great! Another prayer blanket from friends was delivered today. You have so many people who love you, Mom!

CHAPTER 4

Christs Love

February 8, 2012
Ken

Dear Friends/Bible study group,

I had no idea how quickly my life could change! Within less than an hour of arriving at the ER, the doctor explained to me, if I had waited any longer to bring my wife in, the outcome would not have been favorable. He then said, "She will have to be admitted to the ICU unit, be sedated, and have a tube put down her throat into her lungs so she can breathe."

That was an hour that will forever change my life! I have never felt that level of fear and helplessness as I did watching the nurses working on my wife to get her stable. I do not want to create all this drama; I just want my family to know my six-day story.

Two hours of everything going 200 mph, until she was stable. My mind raced with every emotion; some I did not know I had. The reality of what had happened began to sink in. I was numb and not sure what to think or feel. I asked, "God, what do I do?" He said, "Trust me. "I tried! I thought I could manage this all by myself, but that just created more fear.

By this time, they had Kathy knocked out with a mask on her face putting oxygen into her lungs. We were alone in a small, dark treatment room. I looked at her and all the monitors and a feeling came over me like I had never felt before.

I have felt God's presence in my life, but nothing like this. Without a doubt in my heart, I know God said, "You cannot lose what is not yours. Will you love Me if I take My daughter home?"

I realized at that moment I had no control at all. I said, "Yes, Lord, I will love You, no matter what." He gave me a peace in my heart that I can only describe as pure love.

The next couple of days were exceedingly difficult for Kathy, our kids, and me. She fought so hard to breathe, even with the breathing tube. All your texts, emails, and phone calls helped keep me strong. I wish I could talk to all of you, but I am emotionally drained. I really feel your love! You are so special to us! I have seen and been a part of loving other brothers and sisters and even strangers, but when the Lord uses His children to be His hands and feet, it is the best feeling in the world! I love each one of you with all my heart.

I can honestly say I feel the mighty power of prayer in a way I have never felt before. You are all angels, the way you have stepped up and loved us. The Lord is using all of us in ways you would never expect. You have influenced our children with your love and compassion. They have told me how lucky we are to have friends like we do. They are seeing Christ through all of you!

He does not miss opportunities!

Many of you were in the hospital over the weekend praying for Kathy and the kids. Kathy's nurses have been watching all of this. I went out to the nurse's desk to ask her nurse a question and she was crying. I asked if she was OK, and she said, "I want the kind of love your wife has. "I explained to her how we belonged to a large group of friends who have shared their lives with us for many years. I told her how God has shown us, through those friends, the grace, unconditional love, patience, and trust we all need. I know my wife is going to be fine! I have given her to God, and He has given me peace with that.

Thank you for all your help and support. I wanted to come and share all this in person, but my emotions would get in the way. Les and Stumbo would be proud! Turns out that I am quite the crier! Not so much in a sad way, though, but because you all have overwhelmed us with love. Cherish the ones you love; life can change in an instant.

All my love,
Ken

CHAPTER 5

Amber's Journal #2

Wednesday, February 9, 2012, 3:15 PM
Amber

Dear Mom,

 I am feeling a little bit of relief knowing that you are making small improvements. You have now been in ICU for one week. I am praying that your body continues to fight and get stronger every day. Aunt Becci just called to check in on your progress. We just noticed you were starting to respond a little bit. Since they lightened up on the paralytic, you just fluttered your eyelids and coughed. We can now talk to you and touch you; I am so happy, because the past four days they told us not to talk to or touch you. Ken just brought in shoes to keep your feet straight. We all laughed because they were red tennis shoes!

 The doctor came in this morning and said you are maintaining well. He changed two meds and slightly eased up on the paralytic. You are doing well with the adjustments. The nurse today is Shirley.

She just cleaned the inside of your mouth. They do this about every two hours and moisturize your lips. (If you were awake, you would be asking them to put on your LipSense!)

CHAPTER 6

Pleas for Help

Ken

Dear Kathy,

Today you spiked a high fever. The nurses covered you in an ice blanket. This helped bring your temperature down quickly.

Why, God, are You letting her suffer? Why are You putting her through all this stuff? I do not understand. Please stop torturing the two of us! Why are we having to go through all this? Now her heart rate is out of control!

We have all been here at your bedside watching you struggle for ten days (about one and a half weeks). The doctors have put you in an induced coma to help you rest. They have also given you paralytics to keep you from moving. We have all been instructed not to talk to you and not to touch you, and to let you rest. This must be the hardest thing I have ever had to do!

All the kids are at your bedside daily. Shelley has been here since day one, helping all of us understand what is going on with you. I do not know what I would have done without her. She is such an angel! My friend Elias, whom I met in my Bible study group, works here at the hospital, and comes by early every morning to pray over you. He also prays with me and keeps me encouraged.

Everyone we know is praying for you! Everyone wants to come to see you, but there are no visitors allowed in ICU except for family. I made sure of this! The kids, me, and Shelley, all decided you do not need visitors. We also decided we needed to bring in a couple more angels (friends) to be by your side. This way, we can all have a break and take turns watching over you. At this point, it looks like we are going to be here for much longer. Sandy, Toni, and Lori committed to coming in for four-hour shifts.

CHAPTER 7

Amber's Journal #3

Friday, February 11, 2012
Amber

Dear Mom,

You are doing a little bit better each day now. From 8:00 to 10:00 AM, you were breathing on your own. Then you went back on the ventilator all day and tonight, you are supposed to do that again from 8:00 to 10:00. Dr. Hansa says you are maintaining all these changes well. Your eyelids can flutter now, and the nurses say you can hear us. I am hoping you will open your eyes today.

Matt has been here since 9:30 AM. I just got here, and it is 12:30 PM. Ethan has been praying for you every night, Mom. Matt has country music playing right now for you. Shirley is your nurse today. Shelley stayed for quite a while yesterday. It is good to have her here and she likes to be here checking on you every day. If she notices anything different, she talks to the nurse about it and explains everything in detail for me.

Saturday, February 12, 2012

I just got here today, and it is 9:15 AM. Ken is here. We are waiting to talk to the doctor this morning. You went off the vent for one and a half hours this morning and now you are back on. The nurse took you off all sedation for a while and just put you back on morphine. Your heart rate is a little high – 104 right now. The doctor said that is normal because your body is starting to become a bit more aware.

Ken just went home for a while. I talked to Aunt Becci last night, she wanted me to give you a kiss. Kristen has been babysitting the kids for me so I can be here with you.

Monday, February 13, 2012

Dr. Hansa came in this morning and said he wants you to continue to rest all day today and let your lungs heal. He says you must let your body heal and it is going to take time. He put you on Lasix to eliminate the fluids. I got here at about 9:00 AM and I am staying all day until 3:00. Then Shelley comes, and Lori. We are going to let Lori, Shelley, and Sandy come and sit with you for a few hours at a time when we need a break. Chad came by at 6:30 AM to check on you, and he is coming by again at lunch. Matt and Tiffany were here for hours yesterday afternoon. We are hoping and praying you gain strength and healing.

I really miss talking to you, Mom. I love to smell your skin. Matt thinks it's weird, but I get comfort from doing it.

Oh, on Saturday I forgot to write it down: when you were off sedation for a while, I was trying to talk to you and rub my fingers through your hair. I said, "Hi, Mom, I am right here," and you turned your head towards me like you could hear me. That was the only movement we really saw. Later, they turned sedation back on.

Today is seven days that you have been on a ventilator. The nurse did tell us it would be at least seven to ten days. Everyone is praying for you. Ken says people keep calling him for updates on you.

It is raining outside today, but it is starting to clear up. Ethan started his T-ball yesterday, he had a fun time. Whitney Houston died over the weekend (I just thought you might want to know current events).

CHAPTER 8

Out of the Coma and into the Light

Kathy

I woke up three weeks after entering the hospital. I felt like I was coming out of a dream. I wondered, *where am I? What is happening?* Everything was a blur and unrecognizable. *Why are all these people around me?* I drifted back into sleep. Again, I would wake and try to talk, but nothing would come out of my mouth. People were standing around my bed praying over me. *Why are they here and praying over me?* Every time someone came into the room, they would ask me, "Do you know who this is?" I tried hard to think of their name, but my brain was foggy. *What is wrong with me? Why are they in my face? Why do they look so sad?* I can hear whispering going on and nurses talking. Everyone was staring at me, wanting me to wake up and talk to them.

If only I could wake up enough to know all their names and give them a hug and tell them thank you for praying for me!

My whole body hurt, and I could not talk. I was weak as a kitten and felt like I weighed three hundred pounds. I could not move my arms or my legs. I could not even press the call button for help. *Oh, Lord, please help me!*

As the days passed by, my blurry vision left me. Soon, I was able to identify people around me. Then one day, I knew who Bill and Shelley were, but I did not know who my husband was. My poor husband! I was in such a fog for days.

My son Chad was there one day and said to me, "Mom, do you know who this is coming in to see you?"

"Of course, that's my beautiful daughter!"

The days were full of questions from the nurses and my family. I got the feeling that something awful had happened to me, but I did not really comprehend exactly what it was. My sweet husband told me one night, while sitting at my bedside. I could not comprehend what he described. I was in tears! I remember floating in and out of sleep, wiggling my body like a fish, making a chattering sound, and laughing frequently. I also felt pulling and tugging on my body, people screaming, and loud noises. Ken told me months later that the doctors and nurses at that point thought I had brain damage. I was not responding the way they had expected. The doctor sent me to have a brain scan and a CAT scan. Hallelujah, praise the Lord, I did not have brain damage! The drugs must have driven my weird behavior!

I have been awake now for one week and am continuing to improve. The doctors are weaning me off the paralytic drugs. I get an x-ray every day at 6:00 AM. I have breathing treatments twice a day. My oxygen levels are now improving.

The second week after coming out of the coma, the physical therapist came in to evaluate me. I could not talk or move my arms or legs at this point. Being connected to a ventilator for so long had damaged my vocal cords. I answered her questions with a nod of my head, yes or no. My arms and legs felt so heavy as she tried to move them around. Emotionally I was in shock!

The next few days were mentally and physically challenging. Each day I thought, *Today will be the day I can sit up and even stand up.*

The physical therapist said, "Tomorrow, we will sit you up in the 'Cadillac Chair.'" This meant progress to me. Little did I know how horrible 'The Chair' would be!

It is a large metal chair with a little cushion and straps to hold you in so your arms and legs cannot move. A strap goes across your chest, so you do not fall forward. They put me in that chair for five minutes the first time (I could be wrong), and I thought I was going to die! I was so weak and fragile, and my body could not hold a sitting position. I cried and begged (with my eyes) for them to put me back in bed. Every ounce of my body screamed in pain!

"Several days of this chair will help you progress to standing," she said. She was right! I got better at holding myself up and not falling over. Little did I know that all these weeks of lying in bed, having little nutrition, and receiving major drugs to keep me from moving would take away all my muscles!

Why can't I talk? I thought. I was off the ventilator and moving my lips, but no sound would come out. The nurse told me that I had been on the ventilator for a long time and sometimes the vocal cords take time to heal. Everyone was frustrated that they did not understand me. One day, the nurse brought in an alphabet board. She explained that I needed to blink when she pointed to the letter on the board that was the first letter of the word I was trying to say. Then she would be able to spell the words out.

Ken tried, the nurses tried, the kids tried, I tried, nothing worked! All I heard from everyone was, "I don't read lips."

I remember the first time the therapist came in and said, "Kathy, today we are going to sit you on the side of the bed and if you feel OK you can try to stand up." I was thrilled! She brought another therapist with her to help. They sat me up and moved my legs over the side of the bed. They both held me tight, and I stood up. In less than thirty seconds, I passed out!

When I woke up, they were laying me back in the bed. She said, "Are you OK? We will try again tomorrow. Do not get discouraged; this is normal for your first time." I thought about 'tomorrow' all night and prayed God would help me succeed. By the next day, I was feeling determined to sit without passing out. The two therapists arrived with smiles on their faces. They sat me up, and I got dizzy. I sat for a bit longer, and the dizziness went away.

"Now let's try standing," she said. They put a strap around my waist, and both grabbed hold of it, and I stood up. Immediately, my legs gave out and I passed out. However, those few seconds of standing on my feet felt fantastic! I woke up and I was back in bed. Each day after that we tried again. I am not sure how often we tried to stand beside my bed, but I finally got to where I could stand, with a lot of help, for thirty seconds! That meant I could leave ICU and go to the fourth floor! The fourth floor is a step-down unit with wonderful nurses, yet less intensive care. This meant the doctors felt like I was improving enough to move out of ICU. My goal was to finally have more visitors and flowers!

CHAPTER 9

Leaving ICU
Kathy

They placed me right in front of the nurses' station so they could keep a close eye on me. This meant I would be going home soon. I was hopeful! My angels continued to come every day in four-hour shifts. Now that I was on the fourth floor and out of ICU, I received flowers every day – beautiful arrangements and orchid after orchid. I love flowers, but orchids are my favorite. I just could not believe so many people knew I was sick!

One day, my friend Lori Astle, who owns a floral shop here in town, brought in the most beautiful arrangement. She also brought in painted rocks. They are beautiful! Each one has a Bible verse on it. She explained to me that everyone who came into my room could choose a rock to put in their pocket. Lori has been painting on rocks for years now, ever since her nineteen-year-old son died. She has placed rocks on benches and given them out to anyone who wanted one. This is her ministry to others, and a way of helping her through the process of grieving for her son.

We sat and chatted for a while, and Lori asked me if I remembered anything while I was in the coma. I explained to her the only thing I remembered was yelling, screaming, and fighting – people were pushing and pulling on me. She then prayed over me. She asked the Lord to take away all the demons and give me peaceful sleep. As she left, I thanked the Lord for this special angel! I did not share what I heard in my coma with anyone else at the time.

At that point, I had been a fitness therapist and personal trainer with my own business for more than thirty years. My friends and clients were calling Ken and asking if they could visit. Even though this sounded good to me, I knew I was too weak to talk. What I did not know was that my family had decided there were too many people wanting to see me. I was very weak and talking with each visitor challenged my oxygen level. My family thought it would be best if I only had my 'angels' around me. I am thankful now that they made that decision. I was not in any shape to continue a conversation. Plus, every five minutes, a nurse was in my room checking on me or taking blood; the speech therapist was there, or the inhalation therapist, or the physical therapist!

This all meant that I was improving day by day, and I was looking forward to going to rehab.

CHAPTER 10

Hail Mary

March 3, 2012
Ken

Dear Kathy,

Within eight days, a funky, crazy infection got a hold of you, and they could not figure out why. The nurse removed all four PICC lines, and the lab discovered the one in your left arm was infected. You have a major blood infection now. You were complaining that your back hurt.

The nurse came in and said that the doctor had ordered an antibiotic for the infection. She said, "I am going to start the antibiotic and we will be giving your wife a blood infusion." Nancy decided to leave so the nurses could work on you. I walked her out of the building.

I was not gone for ten minutes, but when I returned to the room, they had intubated you, and were rushing you to Imaging! Everyone was upset, telling me you had crashed! As soon as they started the Vancomycin (an antibiotic) for your infection, you went into anaphylactic shock. They had to shock your heart and intubate you. I was furious! I screamed at the nurses for intubating you without me being there.

Imaging showed that your gallbladder was going crazy! Dr. Laughlin (Dr. Hansa's partner in their practice) said, "She is too weak to have surgery on her gallbladder, so I will go in and drain it and see if that helps." Shelley and I waited in the waiting room, praying this would turn you around.

After that procedure, Dr. Laughlin came and told us your gallbladder was full of infection! He did not know why, but the next step he suggested was to start you on a drug called Levophed. He said, "You should prepare yourself, because this is a Hail Mary!" He gave me papers to sign, as this was a last-resort drug to save you. This drug would cut off circulation to your arms and legs and leave everything you needed in your core. The risk was huge! I signed the papers and prayed it would work!

It worked! We moved you back to ICU.

The following days were frustrating for all of us. Levophed had saved your life, but you still had multiple issues to overcome.

As I write this, you are on the ventilator. You have a tracheostomy, a feeding tube in your belly, a catheter in your bladder, and PICC lines in your arms and legs. You had a heart attack when your body went into shock. Your lungs have collapsed four or five times. You have blood clots in your legs. You had surgery to put in an inferior vena cava (IVC) filter to catch any blood clots going to your lungs and heart. You have drain tubes coming out of your lungs.

We are all exhausted emotionally, mentally, and physically!

Spiritually, we are strong!

Our family, our community, and our friends are holding us up in prayer. We pray each day that you will get stronger and be able to fight to live! Dr. Laughlin has explained in detail the side effects of being on Levophed.

Every day I wait patiently early in the morning for Dr. Laughlin or Dr Hansa to show up. They have quite different bedside manners and I get very frustrated with Dr. Laughlin. He comes in and checks on you and goes back to the nurses' station to write his notes on you.

One morning I decided I was going to wait outside your room in hopes he would talk to me before running off to his next patient. I said, "Doctor, can I talk to you for a minute?" He just put his head down and with the politeness that only Dr. Laughlin could give, he said, "OK."

I wanted to know if he would give three minutes of his time and share what he thought that day. He explained, "If I tell you something right now at seven in the morning, by twelve o'clock today, that could be a different circumstance and it could change several times a day."

I told him I understood and would be grateful for just a short conversation. He said, "If you can have that attitude and you understand that I'll brief you when I'm done with her, and you don't bother me while I'm inside, I'll speak with you."

From that point on, we were good, and he kept me apprised of what was going on with you.

Sitting and watching you struggle to survive was the most difficult, heartrending thing I have had to do. My mind was in overdrive! I was thinking, *the Kathy I know prides herself on being fit and healthy! She is rarely sick and when she is, her cheerful outlook helps her recover quickly.* I thought, *wow, she may come out of this a very bitter, angry person! What if she is brain-damaged? What if she cannot walk? What if she has no memory of me? What if she cannot train her clients? What if...*

CHAPTER 11

Meeting Jesus
Kathy

My poor husband had to sign a consent form for them to give me Levophed, a last-resort drug! I am so thankful that I was in a coma and did not know what was going on! As my family sat by my side praying and hoping I would pull through, doctors explained to them if I survived, I might be compromised physically, emotionally, and mentally. He told them I could have brain damage, memory loss, and/or cognitive issues. I might not walk again, and I would have nerve damage in my limbs.

Ken sat in his chair in the corner of my room, praying I would make it. That night – the night after I crashed – was different. I was at death's door. Kelly, my night nurse, came into my room and spoke with Ken and then came over and spoke into my ear.

"Kathy, it is Kelly. You have twenty minutes to live. You need to fight. You need to make a decision to live. If you do not fight, you are going to die. Sweetie, you need to fight now! You have twenty minutes to live!" She repeated these phrases repeatedly.

In my coma, I started yelling, *NO, I do not want to die! I want to live!*

I heard her words, but she did not hear mine. I silently yelled, *Jesus, I need You! Jesus, where are You?* I cried out for Jesus to help me. I sobbed and begged for Him to come. Then, I looked to my right and saw Jesus standing beside my bed.

"I'm here now," he said. He gently picked me up into His arms and held me like a baby. I begged for Him to let me live. "I want more time with my husband. I want to see my grandkids grow up. I want to live! I will do anything You want. Please let me stay." As He cradled me in His arms, stroking my face with His hand, I began to relax. Looking into His eyes, I knew I was His special child. I felt His beating heart with my right ear on His chest. His comforting words took away all my fears.

He said, "Calm down. It is going to be OK; you can stay. You are going to be fine. Rest now. I love you."

He gently laid me back into the bed. I knew at that moment I would be OK! That night, I turned the corner!

I will never forget how Jesus looked at me! His eyes, like sparkling ocean water, are so loving and compassionate. His words, so soft and reassuring. His touch, so gentle, yet strong. Thank You, Lord, for giving me a second chance in life!

CHAPTER 12

Ken's Letter to Angels

Forty-five Days Later
Ken

Hello, my precious church family.

It is early Sunday morning, and I am watching my beautiful wife rest. We are starting our forty-fifth day of this journey that God has us on. I do not understand all the difficulties, all the close calls, or why my precious wife is going through all of this. What I do know is I do not need to, nor am I supposed to understand yet.

God wants us to trust in Him and lay our worries at His feet and let Him bear all our burdens. In the past this would have been extremely hard for me to do. It is not that easy now, but God has brought me to a place of brokenness and surrender. I still feel fear, but I am learning to give it to the Lord, and I know He will use it, and everything else that has hit our group, for His glory – not for our comfort or security. I know whatever God chooses to do will be what brings glory to His kingdom.

Asking God's will for Kathy scares me, but that is my weakness. He has brought me so far in the past forty-five days. He has shown me so much love and mercy and is teaching me patience and trust. So much glory has come from Kathy's illness so far, and I know much more will come. My wife inspires me every day. She is a tenacious fighter, and I am so proud of her. She has amazing doctors and staff in the ICU. Everybody in the unit knows Kathy and they know she is a fighter.

I read something recently that touched my heart. It said, "When we feel the wrench of pain and when we struggle, we can taste the suffering that Jesus endured. It is then His life can be seen in us." I am learning to let go more each day. I cannot stress to you all how much peace our Lord will give us if we just learn to let Him carry us more.

All of you beautiful angels have blessed myself and my family so much; you have no idea what you mean to us and how I love you all. This letter is just a small way for me to thank you for all you do. Knowing you love us and how much you care makes all the difference in the world! Please do not stop, we need all of you. I see Jesus and feel His love through each one of you. You are Jesus's hands and feet. I thank God all day for all of you.

Last weekend was ridiculously hard – we almost lost Kathy, but being the fighter she is, she is more stable now. We have a long way to go, but I know we are going to get through this! That means all of you, too! We are in this together.

I have learned that when you find yourself in the darkness, the enemy wants you. We need to let God walk us through it. I cannot begin to explain how much peace our God will give you if you try and let go. I have had 'God moments' in my life, but nothing like I have had through this! It is pure love and peace. He does not tell me Kathy is going to be OK, but He has shown me I will, and He will never leave me. As hard as this has been, I am grateful at what God is doing to my heart! I cannot wait to see what God is going to do with all of this. It must be something extraordinary! To Him be all the glory!

The enemy messed with the wrong – or right – group of believers, depending on how you choose to look at it, because He will have no victory or glory if we stay strong in the Lord together. You see that someone is hurting, and you get involved. That is mercy! The merciful see a need and try to meet that need. My church family and others have jumped on this like a pack of starving wild dogs on a T-bone steak. You all make God smile!

My prayer for all of you would be: look at your relationships and ask yourself: are you treating each other the way God wants you to? Are you treating our Lord's precious sons and daughters how He would? That is the way He wants us to treat each other. When you see a loved one like Kathy hurting, you realize what is and is not important. It is not what you think it is right now.

My wife is a "10" across the board. But if from now on our house was always a mess; if I never have clean socks or if every dinner she cooks is burnt – you fill in the blank – I will smile and thank the Lord each day for my wife! Honor God with the way you treat His children. If you think you cannot do that and you want to have a relationship that would honor God, then get over it! It is not about you anyway! It is about honoring God and loving each other how He wants us to! So, man up, woman up, and shut up and get to loving each other. I think we would all be shocked at how good that would feel.

I love you all,
Ken

CHAPTER 13

I am Alive!

Kathy

Waking up from the second coma, seeing my husband right next to me, confirmed that I was alive! I drifted in and out of sleep for days, not sure of what was happening or who everyone was. Nothing made sense to me!

As time wore on, my head cleared, and I found out that I had a tracheostomy and a feeding tube, and I was on the ventilator. My doctor had ordered an antibiotic for a blood infection, and I had an allergic reaction. Then a heart attack. Then I was moved back to ICU. The rest is history!

I saw the look in my husband's eyes, how concerned he was, how tired he was, how happy he was that I was awake and alive. All my family were there by my side for so many weeks. They all looked happy that I was awake, but exhausted! How did this happen?

The next few weeks were hard. I could not talk, my vision was blurry, my legs and arms could not move. I was back to square one. Every day, they did an x-ray of my lungs. The respiratory therapist came in three times a day to give me a breathing treatment and suction out my tracheostomy ("trach"). I felt like I was drowning in mucus. I coughed all day and constantly felt like I was choking. I would tell myself, *Tomorrow, I will feel better.*

Slowly my doctor started weaning me off the ventilator. This was a grueling process! My lungs had been functioning using a machine for a long time. Each day, the nurse came in to turn off the ventilator and explain to me what the doctor wanted me to accomplish. "You need to try breathing on your own for fifteen minutes. We need to teach your lungs to work on their own." It was painful! Exhausting! I felt like I was suffocating! My prayer was: *Please Lord, give me relief from all this torture!*

The Lord answered my prayer! Les called Ken and asked if he wanted to be part of the prayer vigil, they were holding that night in the parking lot. Ken needed as much prayer as I did and said yes. Two hours later, Bill and Shelley came to my room. They asked me if they could move my bed closer to the window so that I could see our friends in the parking lot. I immediately started crying.

There I was, coughing my head off, gagging on the mucus in my throat, and Bill was wiping my mouth so gently. Shelley was on the other side of the bed holding my hand tightly. As I looked out the window and saw hundreds of lights shining up toward my room, I sobbed. Bill had his phone turned on so that I could hear the prayers and singing going on. Never in my life had I experienced anything like that moment. The comfort and love I felt that night from our friends continue today.

Amazingly, two weeks later I was off the ventilator and had a Passy Muir Speaking Valve. This valve redirected air flow through the vocal cords, mouth, and nose, enabling my voice to be heard, and improving my communication while swallowing and restoring airway pressure. Since I could not move my hand to my neck, someone else would put a finger over the hole and I could try to talk. Unfortunately, I had no voice.

Dr. Laughlin came in a week later and asked if I wanted to have my trach removed. I was thrilled but scared! My mind went right to having another surgery. Would it be painful? He said, "Let's do it now." He thumped me in the chest and pulled it out! Wow I was in shock! He laughed and said, "There you go! I will order speech therapy and swallow therapy to start tomorrow."

The swallow therapist was a middle-aged (my age) man who treated me like he had known me all his life. He had years of experience and I think was soon to retire. I learned so much every time he came to see me. He gave me thickened water – one teaspoon at a time at first. This was because regular water was too thin, and I would aspirate it into my lungs. I learned to put my chin down first before I swallowed.

He made each day fun. I would try new exercises and swallowing techniques. He would bring new flavors to add to the thick water. My taste buds were gone, so it took a while to wake them up. Slowly I was improving! Within a week of doing this, I graduated to pudding.

Speech therapy came next... at least, that was the plan. To my disappointment, the therapist informed me we needed to wait longer for my vocal cords to heal before we could begin.

Physical therapy was the next order of business. Starting all over again was tough. This time, though, I had an additional challenge – although the Levophed had saved my life by restricting circulation to the core of my body, the lack of blood flow to my arms and legs had left me with gangrene in my feet! My arms were so weak I could not press the call button if I wanted to.

My family and my angels continued to show up, keeping me motivated no matter what I was struggling through. They read to me, bathed me, turned me, called the nurse when needed, and laughed at me. They were the sweetest angels anyone could have. I spent that time hoping someday I could repay the favor!

Day by day, my whisper got stronger, swallowing got better, and my arms and legs started moving. I could hardly wait until I could have a cup of Starbucks! My husband would greet me every morning holding a Starbucks and a scone. They smelled amazing! He would sit beside my bed and turn to the *Animal Planet* channel on the TV. We watched *Escape to Chimp Eden* and Big Cat Diary's together. I love animal shows! He turned the volume low; noise of any kind aggravated me horribly.

Finally, the day came when I could try to swallow hot liquids. He brought me my own cup of Starbucks and a scone. One sip and I almost threw up! It tasted horrible! That was the end of coffee for months.

Days later, my doctor said I could try to eat real food. I was excited to try! Amber came in that day with a curling iron, yoga pants, a T-shirt, and my LipSense. Lunch came, and she fed me small bites. Nothing tasted great, but I was eating! Then she curled my hair, helped me get clothes on, and painted my lips pink! I felt like a new woman!

CHAPTER 14

Leaving the Hospital

April 2012
Kathy

Dear friends, do not be surprised at the painful trial you are suffering as though something strange were happening to you. But rejoice that you participate in the sufferings of Christ, so that you may be overjoyed when his glory is revealed.
(1 Peter 4:12-13 , (NIV)

As I sit in bed this morning, I have mixed feelings about leaving the hospital. This has been my home for sixty-five days (about two months). Even though I have been in a coma, there is a comfort knowing I have had the best care. The nurses and doctors have taken such loving care of me and encouraged me every step of the way. I feel like they are family! They know every part of my body and they know emotionally and mentally what this journey did to me and our family.

I cannot contain my excitement about leaving this hospital and going to HealthSouth Rehabilitation Hospital. I know they will teach me how to move my arms and legs and help me get stronger. But I also realize it is going to be challenging work! I have never in my life felt this weak and disabled. Most people who know me know I love to work hard. So, I am going to live above my circumstances!

God says, "Walk by faith and not by sight."
(See 2 Corinthians: 5-7), NIV.

Finally, the time has come to leave. All the paperwork is complete, and they are taking me downstairs to be transported by ambulance. All my sweet nurses are lined up in the hallway to say, "Goodbye, good luck, stay connected, and let us know how you are doing." I am anxious and teary-eyed.

We arrive at the emergency room and the ambulance is ready. They load me up, hook me up to oxygen, and we are on our way! Ken drives his own truck with my belongings and follows the ambulance. Looking out the back window, seeing his truck following us, brings me to tears, knowing this man has been by my side every day for sixty-five days!

I notice the trees, the flowers, and the colors that spring brings. My heart is full of gratitude that God has brought me this far. Remember, I went into the hospital on February 2, in winter, and it is now April!

CHAPTER 15

HealthSouth Rehabilitation Center

April 2012
Kathy

We arrived at HealthSouth, and I thanked the EMTs who were with me. They had heard stories of my prolonged stay at Memorial Hospital. I did not know that word had spread. Going down the halls to find my room was a feeling I will never forget, I am here! *I am getting better, and this place is going to be a steppingstone to going home!*

The EMTs transferred me to my bed and left. My new nurse came in and talked to me about HealthSouth and all the rules and regulations that come with being in a rehab facility. She said I would not have rehabilitation that day, but they would wake me at 6:00 the following morning for breakfast. The ride over there in the ambulance had exhausted me. All I wanted to do was take a nap!

God said to me, "Do not hesitate to receive joy from Me. Do not let the pain of the past or the worries of the future dominate your mind. Trust Me. I love you."

I had a tough time waking up the next morning at 6:00 AM! Ken arrived around 7:00 AM and helped get my clothes on and feed me. I still had a feeding tube, so I was getting nutrition and I was not very hungry. I was excited for the day to begin!

My therapist, not a strong-looking woman, came in and introduced herself, lifted me out of the bed into the wheelchair, and wheeled me to the gym. *Wow, how did she do that?*

She began the assessment and asked questions, and we discovered my strengths and weaknesses. Even though I had psyched myself up for this day, I was not ready to see the truth. There was much to learn, and I was trying to be courageous, not defeated. Everything she wanted me to do, I failed. As I looked around the room, I realized there were patients worse off than me! At that moment, I promised myself to always look outside myself, to be grateful for where I am and what I can do today!

I went back to my room for rest and lunch, then back to the gym, followed by rest and then dinner. Boy, did I need more energy for that type of schedule! The physical therapy I endured at the hospital involved standing up beside my bed for thirty seconds, and arm and leg exercises that they did for me.

I think one of the best parts about being at HealthSouth is that I could have visitors! From the moment I arrived, I had one visitor after another. My angels came at lunch time to help me to eat. I could not even hold a spoon or put it in my mouth! Each day brought familiar faces that I had not seen in a long time. For unknown reasons, there were friends I did not even recognize. Ken had to remind me who they were. That made me sad.

> *"Let us run with perseverance the race marked out for us."*
> *(Hebrews 12:1, (NIV)*

The first few days in rehab exhausted me to the core! My muscles seemed to have disappeared. I lost fifty pounds in fifty days while in the hospital. My brain told my muscles what to do, but they did not listen. I needed to work hard to wake up my muscles! My brain was tired. My memory issues scared me, too.

Let me tell you: I have spent my whole career as a fitness therapist helping others get healthy and fit. I have trained clients who are in wheelchairs and those who have Parkinson's, Multiple system atrophy, Myotonic dystrophy, back problems, knee problems, shoulder problems, and heart problems, as well as normal, healthy athletes. I know how to encourage and teach them how to get stronger mentally, physically, and emotionally. But I did not know how to be the client or patient. It was hard to put myself in those shoes. Kicking someone else's butt had been my job! I needed to learn to kick my own butt in gear!

> *"My grace is sufficient for you for my power*
> *is made perfect in weakness."*
> *(2 Corinthians 12:9, NIV)*

Each day in the gym, I thought to myself, *how am I going to get from where I am right now to where God is taking me? Every movement is exhausting! But I am not giving up! I will not let the pain of the past or the worries of the future dominate my mind right now. I will do my best to focus on one hour at a time and give it all I have. I will look outside of myself to all the other patients and pray for them. I will live in grat-*

itude for every day that God has given me from this day forward. The Scriptures I shared above kept me focused on God's plans for me.

On day three, the doctor came into my room. He asked, "What would you like to happen first?"

"I would like my catheter out and my feeding tube out."

He explained, "OK. Tomorrow, we are going to take out your catheter. If you eat every meal for the next couple of days, I will take your feeding tube out." I was thrilled to hear this!

The next day, he pulled the catheter out. All I could think about for the next couple of days was getting my feeding tube out. Would it hurt to remove it? Would they sew the hole shut? Would my stomach wall have a hole in it?

Two days later, he came into my room at 7:00 AM and said, "Are you ready to get your feeding tube out?" I asked, "Now?" He said, "Yes, just lay back and relax and it will only take a few seconds."

He pulled my shirt up to expose my belly and yanked it out! I was in total shock. He asked, "Are you OK?"

"Yes, but you could have given me a warning! That hurt!"

He said yanking it out tears the edges of the hole and causes it to heal very quickly.

Now all I needed to do was eat, feed myself, and learn to walk!

Learning to move my arms and legs was incredibly challenging. Trying to get up and stand on two gangrenous feet, with bandages so thick, and pain so piercing, I vomited my guts up! I told myself, *Tomorrow, I will try again!*

Easter weekend came right in the middle of my stay in rehab. Chad brought Brinkley (four years old) and Jagger (eight years old) to visit. They brought a large coloring book and ripped out a page with a giant Easter Bunny on it. They crawled up in bed with me and asked if I could color it with them. Unfortunately, I could not hold a crayon. Jagger grabbed my hand and guided my coloring with Brinkley helping, as well. Chad pinned it on the wall in my room. I will never forget that precious moment with my grandkids. God does not hesitate to bring joy when you least expect it.

My physical therapist spoke with me about my career and family. She heard I was a strong woman before ARDS and reminded me to find the powers within me to move forward. For me, all I had to do was look around the room and see stroke patients, accident victims, and patients with severe disabilities worse than mine. I felt a surge of determination to overcome every obstacle.

Thank God I had no rehab on the weekends! My mind and body were tired! Visitors continued to bless my days and I could now go out to the courtyard.

Beginning the second week in rehab, I was improving in every way. I could hold a fat spoon but could not manage to get the food into my mouth. Family and friends came and helped me with meals; however, after the second week, I was not allowed to have help. I could finally roll on my side. Lifting my arm and bottom one inch off the bed was major progress!

By the end of the second week, I could stand, with help, for two minutes. I learned to move small objects on a table, mostly by sliding them. I could get food to my mouth, spilling it all along the way. My angels teased me and laughed!

One day, my therapist surprised me and put an exercise video on the TV in the gym. She announced to five of us, "You are going to dance today." We were all in wheelchairs, of different ages, and all wanting to learn.

The music came on and my body responded to the beat. She kept encouraging us to move with it. At that moment, I felt alive and happy, no matter what I looked like! It was such a simple exercise video, yet I could not do the moves like the teacher. No one could! Everyone around me kept encouraging me to just have fun. I had not had fun in four months! So, I danced! I found the old Kathy, who loves to dance, at that moment.

By week three, I could walk twenty feet holding on to the parallel bars. Of course, my physical therapist was always holding on to the belt around my waist.

By this time, I could roll over, lift my hips up, reach my arms up to my shoulders, and feed myself. My arms were getting stronger, so I was learning to use a slide board to get out of bed and into my wheelchair. This was the hardest thing to learn! You need strong arms and a strong core, neither of which I had by then. To go home, I needed this skill. I also needed to be able to walk fifty feet with a walker.

My legs felt like twigs with no muscle. My feet hurt 100% of the time. Large bandages made it difficult to put any pressure on them. Gangrene continued to spread. Even so, my time in the acute care rehab facility was limited. Most people stay 10-14 days, due to what insurance will pay. My stay was longer, because I had a fantastic case worker, and I needed more therapy. By this point, I only had three more days to learn the skills I needed. God helped me persevere. I did it! I was ready to leave HealthSouth!

CHAPTER 16

To God Be the Glory!

May 2012
Kathy

Today I can say, "Oh, taste and see that the Lord is good! Blessed is the man who takes refuge in him!" *(Psalm 34:8, NIV)*

Leaving HealthSouth was a day I will never forget! It had been three and a half weeks of arduous work, pain, new beginnings, and overcoming mental, physical, and emotional barriers.

When I was getting ready to leave the rehab facility, my nurse and my sweet husband rushed around getting everything gathered up and ready to go home. As I left the room in a wheelchair, a smile on my face, I was surprised to see all the nurses and staff lining the hallways to say goodbye. They gave me flowers, balloons, and cheers so loud all the other patients could hear them!

I was trembling with excitement and gratitude. This team at HealthSouth taught me to move my entire body, to never give up, to look outside of myself, to overcome every little obstacle in my way.

We were going home! These were words that I had been waiting to hear for ninety days! My whole journey since February 2 had felt like a movie that you would watch on TV. How would it end?

As I am writing today (May 2012), I have learned to color with my grandkids, walk sixty feet with a walker, dance in a wheelchair, and so much more!

My mind is spinning with emotions. *Will I work again? Am I brain-damaged? Will my husband get tired of taking care of me? Will I need surgery on my feet? How long will I be on oxygen? Who am I now if I cannot be a fitness therapist? What does God want me to do now?* God has assured me that He will take care of me and lead me forward.

There have been so many twists and turns, so many friends and family holding us together. Now it is time for homecoming and the next phase of healing! I wonder again: *how will the movie end?* I am not sure of anything, except one thing: God will carry me the rest of the way home!

CHAPTER 17

Be Still and Know that I Am God

Kathy

God said to me every day, "Be still and know that I am God! I will carry you. I will heal you. I have this! I have brought you through the deepest hole and you need to trust in Me and My promises."

When we got home, I could not help but think, *wow, our home is beautiful! The yard looks amazing, and all the flowers are in full bloom.* Remember, I went into the hospital in February when it was winter. Coming home in the springtime was a revelation.

Ken got out of the car and rushed around to get the wheelchair out for me. This was the first time he had to help me get out of the car. We used the slide board and transferred me to the wheelchair. As he rolled me to the front door and we entered the house, I saw the bed – the hospital bed that no one wants to see in their living room!

I knew it was necessary, but I also wanted so badly to sleep with my husband! It had been too long.

He rolled me around the house and out to the backyard. There was a big ugly tree that he had taken out of our yard while I was in the hospital. I remember him asking me before I got sick what kind of tree, I would like to replace it with. I told him I would love to have a magnolia tree. He planted a magnolia tree, which made the whole backyard look more beautiful. I love to garden, and I could not wait until I was able to dig in the backyard.

Next, he rolled me over to the bed and we figured out how to get me into it. Thank God my husband is strong because I was not at that moment!

I was so exhausted from all the excitement of coming home; I was more than ready for a nap! I am sure he was too!

CHAPTER 18

Be Strong and Courageous

May 2012
Kathy

Have I not commanded you? Be strong and courageous!
Do not be terrified! Do not be discouraged, for the Lord
your God will be with you wherever you go.
(Joshua 1:9, NIV)

I have learned to be patient in my affliction. It has not been easy having Ken, my angels, and my children do everything for me. Most days I cry because I am so grateful for their help.

Ken wakes me up in the morning and washes my face and brushes my teeth. His care for me melts my heart! I cannot even explain to you how it feels to have a husband who stands by your side through thick and thin. He loves me no matter how incapacitated I am. I feel his love and compassion deep down inside. He never complains! I see his frustration after an exhausting day at work, but he tries so hard to hide it.

He makes breakfast for me every day and then gives me my drugs. With a kiss and a hug, he is off to work. One of my angels arrives at 8:00 AM to take over my care for the morning. She reads to me, prays with me, changes my bed pan (this is humiliating), listens to me, and then makes lunch for me. My afternoon angel shows up at 1:00 PM. She loves me the same! (How did I get so lucky?) Ken arrives home sometime around 5:00 PM most days. Each night, our friends bring dinner.

While I was in HealthSouth my husband was preparing our home for my homecoming. He is a jack of all trades! He knew that it would be difficult to get me in and out of the shower because of the tile lip, so he built me a shower on the star jasmine-covered patio outside.

He wheels me out to the back patio, undresses me, wraps my bandage-covered, gangrenous feet in plastic, and lifts me onto the shower chair. He fills a five-gallon bucket with hot water and rigs up a showerhead and a pump. He bathes me with tenderness. We both laughed so hard the first time we used it. He had thought of everything!

Day after day, I lie in my hospital bed, looking out the French doors and dreaming of the day I can walk and do things for myself.

We have a Ficus tree just outside the French doors. One day, a hummingbird started making a nest in the tree. I watched each day as it meticulously built a cocoon for its babies. I love hummingbirds! Watching Mama Hummingbird, I thought of how God has prepared me for this journey. He has held me in His arms, comforted me through every procedure, and built a beautiful community to hold us up. He has given me a purpose to live my life to the fullest, and to glorify Him in everything!

For two weeks, I watched Mama Hummingbird build her nest. I felt the struggle she was going through. I felt the anticipation of when the nest would be completed. I knew God had given me this example as a sign of what was to come.

To my shock, one day Mama Hummingbird started taking her nest apart! I was so sad for her and for me. Was there something God was trying to tell me? The only words I heard from Him were, "Be still and know that I am Lord."

Every day, I prayed He would give me courage to persevere. I asked Him to heal my feet so I would not need surgery. Every week, I went back to the hospital for wound care. Dr. Sinai (my foot surgeon) gave me no hope my gangrenous feet would heal. He wanted me to have surgery to amputate my toes. Every visit back to the hospital to see him depressed me.

Home care was set up to come to my house every other day to change my bandages. Week after week, the pain grew worse. The smell of gangrene was horrible! I just knew if I gave it more time my feet would heal. After two months at home, my baby toe fell off while the dressing was being changed. I knew it was time to go back to the hospital. Fear crept into every part of my being! Ken prayed with me. My angels prayed with me. I gave my fear to the Lord. My faith in Jesus took over! He promised me that I would be fine; that He would take care of me, no matter what! So off to the hospital we went.

CHAPTER 19

Mount Up with Wings Like Eagles

July 2012
Kathy

But they who wait for the Lord shall renew their strength, they shall mount up with wings like eagles; they shall run, and not be weary; And they shall walk, and not faint. (Isaiah 40:31, NIV)

This has been my life verse for twenty-five years.

Ken
Surgery Day

Dear Kathy,

    After your toe amputation surgery, Shelley and I were there in your room waiting for you to arrive. When they rolled you into the room, you were screaming in pain! I asked the nurse to please get the doctor. She explained that you had pain medication in surgery.

A doctor I had never seen before came into the room and said he was the hospitalist (doctor) on call. He said, "She has already been given pain medication in surgery and that was all that she could have." I was furious and told him I was calling Dr. Hansa. I wanted to know, "Have you read her chart so you can know what medication she is on every day for pain?" He had not!

I told the nurses at the station that I did not want that doctor in my wife's room ever again. I called Dr Hansa. He must have been close by because he came into the room seconds later. I told him what had just happened. "Please help her!"

He said, "This is ridiculous. "He gave orders for more medication to be given. Dr. Hansa then sat down with Shelley and me for more than an hour. He never took his eyes off you and watched as you began to relax and sleep. We all sat there talking about his life and all that we had overcome in the last six months. He is the most compassionate doctor I have ever been around!

The hospitalist, who had been so rude and uncaring, came back into the room after Dr. Hansa left. He was upset that I had forbidden him access to you. At that moment, I did not care what he thought or felt; he was not to come back into your room.

From that point on, Dr. Hansa made sure to check in on you frequently and make sure you were not in severe pain. This surgery brought you, mentally and physically, to a new level of pain.

Each day, Dr. Sinai came in to check on you. He would say, "It takes time to heal from a surgery like this, hang in there."

Home Again
Kathy

"Four months with no pressure on your feet," Dr. Sinai said. "You do not want the incisions to break open. Remember, do not get your feet wet. Keep them elevated," he repeated. "I'll see you in a week."

I left the hospital a week after seven of my toes were removed due to gangrene. The next four months are a blur! More pain medication, more prayer, more angels, more lying around letting everyone else take care of me. I grew restless. I had too much time to just lie in my bed, with my feet up, thinking. Then I would remember the book that Lori had brought me: *It's Not About Me!* by Max Lucado.

How can I inspire others? How could I not wallow in my pain? How could I endure this struggle with grace? Max wrote, "My pain expands God's purpose." I need to move from 'me-focused' to 'God-focused'!

Month after month, I visited the wound care center at the hospital to make sure I was healing properly. Four months after the surgery, Dr. Sinai said it was time to take the stitches out. I was apprehensive, to say the least. He explained to me it might hurt just a little, so he would be quick to get them out. Ken was standing right beside me, holding my hand.

The minute the doctor started taking the first stitch out, I screamed in pain. He looked at Ken and said, "You'll need to hold her down." Ken lay on top of me while I screamed and begged the doctor to stop. I still remember that day, vividly: the pain, the look on Ken's face, how trapped and tortured I felt! I will never forget that moment!

Time passed slowly as I continued to heal.

CHAPTER 20

Ken's Precious Words

August 2012
Ken

Dear Kathy,

As time went on, I saw how Christ molded you! He changed your focus to see His perspective. Your heart has changed, and I never saw you angry about your situation, not even once! You embraced every day and gave God all your worries. You cannot help but live for a purpose much greater than yourself. God just filled your cup over with HIS love! You experienced a miracle and you have done nothing but honor Him every moment since! My beautiful wife is still there but God did a 'one-eighty' in your heart! You still have the same drive and determination, but you are using it to heal! Your career – your passion to help people – has been who you are!

Now, I know you lie in bed and think about your clients every day, but you realize you need to rest and find out who you are through this journey, without working full-time!

CHAPTER 21

Blessings from God
Kathy

My mother once told me that in life, if you are lucky, you can count on one hand the number of close, intimate friends you will have in a lifetime.

I remember sitting in her living room one day asking her how she got so many friends. She explained to me that it was especially important to have friends in all areas of my life. She had friends at church, in her work as a nurse, at the chamber of commerce, at Bible study, and of course, her bridge group. She told me I should have friends that were my age, older, and younger. She said when you get old, and all your friends are old, they all get health problems and die. But if you have younger friends, they inspire you to stay younger!

You see, I had always wanted to be like my mom. As we continued to talk about girlfriends, I explained to her that I wished I had close girlfriends. I hoped I would find friends that were like-minded – ladies I could trust and share life with. I was always the girl who hung out with the boys because I did not like how gossipy and petty the girls were. I guess you would say I was always an independent child, but now in the middle of my life, I was craving those close friendships with women!

I began praying every day for God to give me girlfriends I could do life with; girlfriends I could love and be myself with. I wanted deep relationships that were reciprocal.

I also prayed that my husband would find friends who could mentor him. Friends he could talk to on a gut level. Godly men who could hold him accountable.

God has blessed us tenfold! He has given us both friends who love unconditionally. He has graced our life beyond what we could have imagined. He initially gave us a small Bible study group to join (six couples). These couples needed more of Jesus, just like us. We gathered each week to pray, study the Bible, share our personal stories, do community service projects, study books on marriage, and learn more about Jesus! This group eventually became a large group of fifty couples over a period of ten years.

We call these friends 'angels.' They were there before, during, and after my hospitalization. They are the hands and feet of Jesus! They put their life on hold to be at my bedside. They prayed fervently that God would heal me. They planned prayer vigils in the parking lot at the hospital. They held my family members' hands and prayed for them through tough days. They read to me at my bedside even when I was in a coma. They helped bathe me, turn me, and massage lotion into my body when the nurses needed help. They spent long hours at the hospital and never complained. They brought a smile to my face and a warm, fuzzy feeling to my heart. They were the gatekeeper to my room and a messenger to the outside world. They are family!

On that first night in the emergency room, as my husband was receiving my diagnosis of ARDS, our angels gathered around. From that moment forward, they stood beside our family in support, offering whatever they needed! I would not be here today authoring this book without all our friends and their prayers, time, and encouragement.

CHAPTER 22

Our Community Gathers

Kathy

Our kids set up a "Fun Run Fundraiser" held at our church on March 24, 2012, while I was still in Memorial Hospital. Everyone signed a large, framed photo of me with encouraging words. Friends set up tables to sell their merchandise. There was a BBQ and auction items to bid on.

The fundraiser brought in $27,000 to offset our medical bills! When I woke up and was able to see this large picture and all the signatures on my wall, I cried in amazement. Family, friends, and people I did not even know all ran for my life!

Our friends also had a Cinnamon Roll fundraiser to help with our expenses.

My sister, who lives in Charleston, South Carolina, started a GoFundMe page. She hoped that all our friends around the USA would give a donation. These funds helped pay our bills and bless us beyond our imagination.

My brother Eric set up a Caring Bridge website, and my kids wrote updates so everyone would know how I was progressing. This also helped friends know exactly how to pray.

> *"I lift my eyes to the hills. Where does my help come from? My help comes from the Lord, the Maker of heaven and earth."*
> *(Psalm 121:1-2, NIV)*

CHAPTER 23

The Love of Grandkids

Kathy

Remember the rocks Lori brought me when I was in the hospital? Well, Amber and her family went to the beach for the weekend and Ethan kept looking for a rock. He brought one home, gave it to me, and asked me if I would write on it for him.

"What do you want me to write?" I asked.

"Can you write that you love me to the moon and back?" (This is what I say to all the grandkids when we say goodbye.) "Can you write that Jesus loves me?" he asked. "Don't forget to sign it, Granny."

My sweet grandson had learned the power of Scripture on rocks. I had regular visits from all the kids and grandkids for the whole summer. They rode on my lap in the wheelchair, took naps with me, played in the pool, and filled my heart with joy.

CHAPTER 24

Frustration Arises

Kathy

It has been seven months now since I have been lying in a hospital bed. I am sure you can only imagine how weak I am. At this moment, I am feeling very depressed and caged in! Since the surgery on my feet, my doctors have not given me permission to start physical therapy yet, so, I wait, and hope for the day to come soon.

My feet are healing, my arms and legs are getting stronger, but my appetite is gone! Nothing really tastes good. All I can think about is working out and moving my muscles. I keep telling Ken that I do not need babysitters all day every day! He says, "You are not ready yet, babe. You still need everything."

I love my husband and all that he does for me, but I am getting really irritated with him. I just want to be independent! I need to go back to physical therapy. *Please Lord, help me.*

CHAPTER 25

My First Speaking Engagement

August 23, 2012
Kathy

Learning to Walk on Faith that Hurts.

My friend Nancy invited me to speak in front of Community Bible Study leaders at her home. They are a large group of women who have prayed for me since the beginning of my journey. Nancy is the leader of this group and has been for twenty-eight years. That day was also my mom's birthday. She had passed the year before and never knew about my illness. I honored her that day by sharing my story. She always cheered me on when I had speaking engagements in the past. I knew she was cheering for me from Heaven.

This was also the first day I was able to put on sandals, even though I could not walk yet. Shelley (my angel) was so excited for me and this opportunity that she came over and painted my three toes! She drove me to Nancy's house and recorded my presentation.

All the women were so happy to see me. As I sat on the hearth of the fireplace sharing my story, my heart was full of emotion. Tears flowed with gratitude that God chose me to be here today! He blessed me with a large community of Jesus-seeking friends and prayer warriors. I walked away that day feeling loved beyond my imagination. Driving home with Shelley, hearing her insights of the morning, filled my heart with God's purpose for me.

CHAPTER 26

Back to Rehabilitation

September 12, 2012
Kathy

Today, I was extremely happy to be able to start my first day of rehabilitation since my doctor removed my toes. My therapist was Tonya, a cute young woman with a great personality. After a full assessment, we started on the stationary bicycle. I was still on oxygen, so she had to be incredibly careful about watching my O_2 levels. "We are going to just take it slow, one day at a time, and you are not to overdo it," she explained.

Trust me, after three minutes on the bicycle, I was dying and had to stop! After three more exercises, I was exhausted! When I returned home, I slept for two hours! All I could think about that night was, *I need more painkillers!*

October 2012

I am continually weaning off the oxygen now and doing very well. Dr. Hansa says my lungs are improving. I have been going to physical therapy for three weeks now and after a rough start, have been loving every minute of it. I wish Tonya would make my workouts harder. I know what my body is capable of, and I am in a hurry to get back to full activity! Tonya is concerned about my oxygen levels, risk of falling, and my increase in pain post workout.

Today, I told Tonya, "I am bored with my workouts. I want to do more exercise. I can endure the pain."

"That is not what you should be doing... ever!" she said.

My personality is to overcome all obstacles to get to where I want to be, now! Unfortunately, I need to change my mindset, adapt to a new one, and accept a slower pace for recovery!

Who am I? Am I really this stubborn? Lord, help me live one hour at a time. Cast away my old attitudes and guide me to the place You want me to be.

November 2012

Goodbye, oxygen tank! Workouts are getting harder and more satisfying. However, my feet are killing me! It is like a double-edged sword: I need to get stronger, but I want less pain. Now that I am using all my muscles and challenging them, my appetite is improving. Yay! This sounds crazy but I am learning to walk on faith that hurts!

December 2012

I love you, Oh Lord, my strength!
(Psalm 18:1, NIV)

Yes! God is healing my weak body! There is now a challenge every time I go to rehab. Because of my training and experience, I have decided to add in different exercises that I know will help. Tonya is OK with it, but she continually reminds me to be careful.

I mentioned earlier that I lost fifty pounds in fifty days while in the hospital. I have spent my entire life building muscle, staying strong, and after my hospital stay, I had NO muscle and sagging skin! I keep telling myself, *this is temporary! I will make muscle!* Thankfully, this saggy body is finally firming up and feeling stronger! My angels keep complimenting me, on how much better I look. My color has improved, my skin is firming up, and I have more enthusiasm for life! It has always amazed me how you can work your muscles, with no dieting, and your body gets tighter and firmer! My appetite is still not up to par. I hate drugs! Unfortunately, I need them.

CHAPTER 27

My Birthday

December 17, 2012
Kathy

It is my fifty-seventh birthday! I am walking, talking, eating, exercising, and feeling blessed beyond measure! Ken and I were invited to go to the beach this weekend to celebrate. The beach is my favorite place in the world! Greg and Toni's beach house is on the top of the mountain in Avila Beach, California. It has multiple levels, with views of the ocean and mountains. Bill and Shelley joined us.

For my birthday weekend, we talked, laughed, cooked wonderful food, and went to the beach. Even though I could not walk on the sand yet due to my incisions, we could still smell the ocean and listen to the waves. When we arrived at the boardwalk, Ken helped me out of the car and into the wheelchair. We all strolled down the boardwalk, enjoying the fresh air and sunny skies. The vibe in Avila is casual and happy.

Everyone stopped when we got to the staircase that led down to the sandy beach. Then the most beautiful thing happened: Bill and

Greg picked me up and carried me down onto the sand! Ken stepped back and watched from behind, in awe of what our dear friends were doing. They set up chairs and umbrellas, sat me down in the chair, and covered me from head to toe with beach towels. I had not been in the sun for more than a year! I was also on drugs that made me sensitive to the sun.

We enjoyed lunch on the beach. They had thought of everything. The weekend was perfect in every way!

CHAPTER 28

One Year After ARDS

February 2, 2013
Kathy

Wow, it has been one year since I entered the hospital! Our dear friends Les and Lori (leaders of our small group) own a home at the beach. This beautiful home sits on a quiet golf course just a short drive from the ocean. They offered me the opportunity to stay there for a couple of weeks.

Bakersfield has fog and bad air quality this time of year. I struggle with my asthma from December to March because of the mold in Bakersfield. Christmas trees arrive in early December and carry the most amount of mold a tree can have. Add in fog and rain, and I start wheezing.

I feel blessed beyond words to be able to have time alone and great air! Ken usually comes over on the weekend and we enjoy walking on the beach. This is a place where I can sleep twelve hours a night, journal my deepest thoughts, enjoy nature, and focus on what God wants me to do next.

This past year has been the hardest year of my life! God has transformed me from death to life. He gave me – a broken woman, full of sin and attitude – a second chance at life. I believe when we face our own personal giant-sized dilemma, we need to remember that the giant is never bigger than God.

"The one who is in you is greater than the one who is in the world."
(1 John 4:4, NIV)

He is always victorious!

It is not our circumstances that hold us back, but our attitudes in those circumstances. Through every situation over the past year, I have never been angry at God. I have never asked Him why this happened to me. This place to which God has called me brings deep gladness and a hunger for what I can learn from it all. Friends ask if I am depressed. I tell them no, but I am sure I have had pity party days and moments of depression. I do not camp out there for long. Someone once told me "The seeds of depression cannot take root in a grateful heart." When all this happened to me, I somehow knew God's plan for me was bigger than I could ever imagine!

"We know in all things God works for the good of those who love Him, who have been called according to his purpose."
(Romans 8:28, NIV)

On this special day, one year after I collapsed, I am walking on the beach, breathing clean air. I see footprints in the sand and Jesus holding my hand every step of the way. There is nothing more healing than being in my favorite place!

CHAPTER 29

Dependent on Drugs
Kathy

I never imagined in my wildest dreams that I would be writing about being dependent on drugs! Now, one year later, I am still frustrated with being on so many.

I was taught at an early age to never take drugs unless you absolutely needed them. My mom was a Registered Nurse and encouraged us kids to "tough it out." Well, I need the drugs now to get through every day, whether I like it or not!

I wear a fentanyl patch that is replaced every three days. I take OxyContin every four hours. I need an anti-inflammatory drug, anti-anxiety drug, and something for neuropathy in my hands and feet. I also need another drug to sleep. All these drugs kill my appetite! I feel nauseous every day all day. I have memory loss – short-term and long-term. *Please Lord, help me get off these drugs!*

Slowly, my appetite has returned after more intense physical therapy. My memory has started coming back.

Six and a Half Years Later

Little did I know then that for the next six and a half years, I would be on a rollercoaster of drugs and pain. Every month, I would visit my pain management doctor. This doctor was assigned to me when I left the hospital. I would sit in his smelly, disorganized office for hours, even though I had a set appointment. When he came in and sat down to speak with me, he would never look at me. His eyes were always on my chart while asking me questions: "What is your pain level today? What is your average pain level? Do you need more drugs? What do you need refilled?" Then he would hand me my prescriptions and walk out.

I would make my next appointment and leave feeling uncared for. I could not get to the pharmacy quickly enough. Fentanyl patches and OxyContin were two controlled drugs I took for pain. I could not refill the prescription until the day I ran out of them. My anxiety level, my fear of pain, and the possibility of the pharmacy not being able to fill my prescription put me on edge every month!

If you have never been on drugs, you cannot comprehend how horrible it can feel emotionally, mentally, and physically. I felt emotionally exhausted all the time! I thought, *why am I not able to control my pain?* Mentally, I felt defeated! Physically, I felt like I was dragging a one-hundred-pound dumbbell around behind me.

Our friends and family always asked, "How are you? How is your pain?" I would think about the question for a minute and then answer, "I'm good and the pain is getting better." Positive thinking always makes me feel better. But my eyes, the window to my soul, spoke differently. Year after year, I had improved on a physical level; mentally, I had become stronger; emotionally, I had become more introverted and less likely to share my pain. Drugs do this to you, whether you like it or not!

My opioid crisis began after four years of being on opioids. I needed more to control my pain. Drugs never took my pain away; they just took the edge off. During one office visit, my pain management doctor explained that he would not be able to continue to give me more because the government was cracking down on opioid prescriptions. "Too many people are using and abusing these drugs," he said. I was frustrated with his lack of compassion and continued to pray for a new direction and a new doctor. I called five other pain management doctors here in town and no one was accepting new clients.

CHAPTER 30

New Opportunities at USC

May 2018
Kathy

In May 2018, I decided it was time to change my direction. After six and a half years, all I could think about was taking my pain-relieving drugs every four hours. Pain ruled my life! Every time I changed my fentanyl patch (every three days), I would pray that I could sleep through the night without waking up in pain. That never happened! I never felt high or out of pain.

One morning, I had had enough! I called my family doctor, whom I had not seen in seven years because I had so many other doctors caring for me. I made an appointment. I prayed all the way to the doctor's office, hoping he would have answers for me.

To my surprise, my doctor did not come in, but a handsome young nurse practitioner did. He introduced himself and said he had read my chart. "Wow, you are a miracle! How can I help you? "

I told him I was sick and tired of being on drugs that controlled my life. I briefly explained my situation and asked if he knew of a new direction I could take. He asked, "Why are you still searching in Bakersfield?"

"I do not know. I feel stuck! I have tried to find other pain management doctors here in Bakersfield, I suppose for convenience, but they were not taking new patients."

"I would like you to go to USC to the best pain management doctor in the United States," he said, referring to the Keck Medical Center at the University of Southern California.

"Why USC? "

"I trained there," he said. He told me he could get me an appointment within a week. I was shocked! My prayers were being answered! When I got in the car to go home, I cried, knowing I was starting on a new journey of pain relief. *Thank You, Jesus, for answered prayer!*

USC called me the next morning to schedule an appointment for the following week. Every day, I prayed this would be my fresh start! I arrived at my appointment and Dr. Faye Weinstein walked into the room with a smile on her face and a gentle heart. She is a pain psychologist. She asked me a thousand questions in the two hours we were there. She recommended I see Dr. Steven Richeimer, the head of the pain management department. She said she would set the appointment up and after I spent time with him, she would see me again.

Ken and I left the hospital that day feeling hopeful! We talked about the questions that she asked me. We prayed that if this were the right doctor and the right hospital, God would confirm every step of our journey.

One week later, I met Dr. Steven Richeimer. In my research he truly was "the god of pain management in the whole USA!" I was excited to meet him and hear what he had to say.

Dr. Richeimer walked into the room with one of his "Fellows" and introduced himself. I immediately felt his compassion and his kind, gentle soul. He has the eyes of an angel! He explained that he teaches with a team of doctors who would collaborate on my case, and we would need to drive to USC often to see him and his team. He asked me what I wanted to happen first. "I want off opiates and the fentanyl patch, ASAP! "

He left the room to speak with his team and came back with a plan. The first thing I needed to do was wean off these drugs slowly. He would guide me through the process month by month and would not replace the drugs with any other drugs. Mentally, I was ready for the next step, but physically, I was scared! Emotionally, I knew I could do it with God's help.

Dr. Richeimer and his team asked me to come down monthly for various tests. First would be a full physical. He said if I passed all the tests, he thought I could be a candidate for their ketamine infusion program. They explained the program to Ken and me. We sat in silence, listening to all the hoops I would need to jump through to be a part of this program.

He explained that he had started the program seven years prior. So far, he had had incredibly promising results for patients who stuck with the program and did everything he said. He advised us of what I needed to have in place:

I would need to be clean of opiates and fentanyl within one year.
My start date would be March 4, 2019.
I would need to live close to the hospital for three or four months.
I always needed someone with me.
I needed a driver to and from the hospital.
I needed to be cleared by my cardiologist.
I needed my pulmonologist to clear me for the program.
I needed to see Dr. Weinstein four or five times before I could start the program.
I needed to see the foot specialist at USC.

I needed to understand that the side effects would be incredibly challenging.
I needed all my prayer warriors if I wanted to get through this program.

OK. So, the last one was not Dr. Richeimer's, but it was just as important for me as the others.

We were completely overwhelmed by all this information; however, we knew that God had set us on this path, and we would succeed! Look at what He had already done! Our faith was strong. I was more determined than ever to get off those drugs. We both knew that our family and friends would step up and help. *Please, Lord, if it be Your will, help us navigate each of these steps and be accepted for this program.*

Each week, the detox protocol got harder as my pain increased. I became more reclusive. I did not want to talk about my pain, and I did not want anyone to see my pain. My determination to succeed got stronger!

Having a compassionate, loving husband holding my hand every step of the way made me more determined than ever. He watched me change right in front of his eyes, month after month. I am not a complainer when it comes to pain; I tend to retreat inside myself so no one can see how I am feeling. However, Ken saw right through me! My family and friends saw pain in my eyes and in how I walked. I prayed often for God to release me from all the pain, to help me persevere through the detox and not give up.

I went to see Dr. Weinstein four more times. She spoke with me about my mental and emotional state after going through so much trauma. She explained how the sympathetic nervous system works and gave me tools to start taking better care of myself. This system in our bodies controls 'fight or flight' responses. "The parasympathetic nervous system restores the body to a state of calm." I had not been in a state of calm for seven years by then.

I thought of all those years I had been taking diligent care of my health and my body. I did yoga, ate right, prayed, and did deep breathing exercises daily. I explained to the pain psychologist how all these tools I used helped me and helped my clients.

She asked me one question that threw me for a loop: "Kathy, why are you so good at taking care of others, using all your tools in your toolbox, but yet you don't take care of yourself?" Wow, that hurt! I burst into tears and could not speak. She told me to go home and think about this question.

She also wanted me to start "gaming" on my computer when I was feeling severe pain. What? I was not a gamer, but I said I would try. I tried for months and decided *I am not a gamer!* I felt like I was wasting time and I could benefit from doing something else. She advised me to sit down and put my feet up if my pain level was over a four, with ten being the worst.

I love to read books and listen to podcasts, garden, and exercise, so that is what I did to divert my thoughts about my pain. Did it work? Temporarily! I thought, *my pain today does not predict the future!* I needed to learn to dance (or walk) to new music, create innovative ideas, and make new choices to get through all the pain. If I wanted to hear the tune of the music, I had to stop talking, stop trying to persuade myself, and listen to Dr. Weinstein.

Those four sessions with my pain psychologist made me think deeper about pain and dysfunction. She gave me insight into how I was not giving myself grace to just rest in it. We all have a 'fight or flight' response to painful stimuli, and like she implied, I wanted to fight with every tool in my toolbox! I now knew I had to change my mode of operation.

CHAPTER 31

My Ketamine Journey

March 4, 2019
Kathy

I made it through the detox, and I started infusions on March 4, 2019! I was focused and ready to succeed! I was also nervous about how my body would respond to the ketamine infusions.

Please, Lord, do not let the pain of the past or the worries of the future dominate my mind! Self-talk and listening to podcasts became my go-to. On the first day of my infusions, one of my nurses gave me a link to a forty-five-minute prayer on YouTube that she thought would relax me. From that day forward, when I get an infusion, I listen to it. With a smile on my face and warmth in my heart, I fall asleep. Look on YouTube for "The Best Sleeping Music and Prayer How to Get Healing-By Susan Richards.

My whole purpose in life is to glorify God in everything I do. When you are in severe pain, and you do not want everyone to know, how do you use this to glorify God? The answer came to me months into this journey: I was to be honest and real. I was to be humble and open. I was to ask for prayer every step of the way!

I told myself to inhale and exhale… and smile! I have always been a person who smiles often, even through painful circumstances. Someone once told me that smiling can be an act of defiance, an act of bravery, or an act of brokenness. I will continue smiling because I have so much joy in my heart. I will live in gratitude, no matter what!

"Do not hide your light! Let it shine brightly before others, so that the commendable works will shine as his light upon them, and they will give their praise to your father in heaven. "
(Matthew 5:16, TPT)

Our friends and family gave generously to help us secure an apartment close to USC. We lived in this beautiful apartment for three months. We drove thirty-five minutes to USC early every morning. I received infusions every day for four and a half hours. Most days after the infusion, I was Gumby! I had double vision, could not walk well, and felt drunk.

My brother Monte and his wife Marilyn called to say they were flying out for the first week to help. They cooked each meal with love, laughed at me for being out of control, drove me to and from the hospital, and loved me unconditionally. My brother Eric came three weeks later to help. We sent out a calendar and asked our friends to come help if they had time. During those months of infusions, sweet family time and friends coming to help made a dramatic difference in my pain level. I lost all control of everything in my life. But God provided everything we needed!

This whole journey has taught me that I am not in control of anything; that God's grace is what gets us through life.

Having family and friends who love you enough to do the hard things for you – things like driving me to and from my infusions, staying with me when I was 'out of it,' cooking for me, encouraging me to persevere through all of it – that is love! I put one step in front of the other each day, knowing God has given me a miracle. He loves me. He has resources beyond my imagination! He wants to carry us, and He wants us to give Him all the glory!

I have been traveling to USC for ketamine infusions for three and a half years now. I am on a six-week rotation and have experienced good pain relief. My husband or my girlfriends drive me down to USC, we stay overnight, I have my second infusion the next day, and we drive home. The best part is, I get to spend alone time with my girls (my angels)! My doctor is not sure how long I will need these infusions, but we will continue until they are not working anymore.

Today, September 2023, I enjoy life one day at a time. I feel vibrant and healthy! I am able to work part-time with my clients. I walk, dance, swim, and practice yoga with pain. My feet hurt 24/7. This pain reminds me every day of how far I have come since 2012. I used to play all sports, but today running and jumping create too much pain. When our grandchildren want me to play basketball or soccer, I join in; however, I pay the price with pain! I am so grateful to be alive and able to play with grandkids!

Mentally I feel sharp although I have some long-term memory issues. The nerves in my hands and feet are on fire most of the time. Sleeping is a challenge with pain and nerves on fire. Thank You, Jesus, for non-habit-forming drugs that help!

My lungs have healed incredibly well! I do breathing exercises every day to keep them strong. My asthma kicks up two or three times a year and quickly gives me an infection. I do have scarred lungs from ARDS, which makes my lungs extremely sensitive when I have asthma issues. I love to garden and be outside as often as I can. Bad air quality and fumes from candles, detergents, air fresheners, smoke, and altitude bother my lungs. I Love to travel anywhere! I love yoga. I love to go to my grandkid's sports events. Most of all, I love waking up with my precious husband next to me. I am a Fitness Therapist and have the pleasure of working with my clients daily. My heart is full of Joy and Jesus made all this possible!

We are actively involved with our small group (Bible study) weekly. In 2012, our group was large (fifty couples). Two years ago, the group split into many small groups. The friends we had when this journey started are friends today. They continue to bless our life!

God placed me exactly where I am supposed to be, facing these challenges, and filled with hopes and dreams of being completely healed!

CHAPTER 32

What Have I Learned from the Last Eleven Years?

Kathy

Embrace life as if you were a child.
Have fun, try new things, go to unfamiliar places, meet new people, and sing for Jesus.
Engage your children and grandchildren in conversations that inspire them. Teach them about Jesus!
Be active and get out of your own way.
Believe in miracles!
Break every chain that is binding you.
Read your Bible and/or devotional daily and keep your mind on Jesus.
Do your best in everything that you do.
Let go and let God guide your life.
Learn to be humble.

Live like there is no tomorrow.
Give from your heart to everyone around you.
Grow in your purpose and run with endurance the race that is set before you.
Slow down and be intentional.
Invest in other people and relationships.
Share your story for His glory.
Listen more to those around you.
Rise above your circumstances.
Pray for every little thing and every important thing. Pray that God would use you for His glory!

"Be still and know that I am God."
(Psalm 46:10, NIV)

"Always believe in miracles!"

I desperately want to live in such a way that one day, I can look back and wonder at all the "God things" He did in and through my life. I pray that those who come behind me will celebrate what God can do for them after watching what He has done for me! I have lived an extraordinary life that God planned out for me. He never said it would be easy through my own power but promised through Him – through God's power – all is possible!

I have learned that sharing everything in marriage matters. When Ken and I got married twenty-six years ago, we each owned our own business. We kept our business bank accounts separate. We had one joint account and a savings account. We were both very independent, scarred by past marriages, and determined to make our marriage work. I never thought of having him be a cosigner on my business account, or me on his.

When I entered the hospital, my business stopped, my income stopped, and his income changed. He was at my bedside taking care of my every need. When he came up for air and realized the household bills needed to be paid, the bank would not let him into my account. He had access to our joint account, but not mine. He did not have passwords for any of the bills online. He did not have a PIN or a debit card of mine. I was the one who took care of paying all our bills. Somehow, weeks later, because of prayer, the bank let him have access. God opened the doors for him to get help! Not only did the bank help, but our family and friends supported us financially.

Months later, after I got home from the hospital, I was ashamed! Why had I not had him cosign on my account years ago? I could not work or make an income anymore. We had bills pouring in from every doctor who had touched me, with hospital bills so daunting and overwhelming, all I could do was cry.

I still needed full-time care at home and my husband was working as hard as he could to make up for lost time. I prayed, "Lord, lead us in the right direction. Provide us with someone who can help." Within five days, one of my angels (Robin) helped me write letters to every doctor and to the hospital. In every letter, we told my story of sixty-five days in Memorial Hospital. We asked for forgiveness or a reduced amount to pay. We prayed over every letter that God's will would be done. God answered our prayers tenfold! Half of the bills were forgiven, and the other half reduced their fees! Hallelujah, praise the Lord!

Lesson learned: always share your passwords with someone you trust, make sure you cosign for each other's accounts, and save extra money for 'when your life changes in a second.'

CHAPTER 33

Prayer Works
Kathy

Prayer is a gift! You should give it and ask for it. You just never know who wants a blessing or wants to give you a blessing. Hundreds of times over the last eleven years, I have been approached by someone I did not know, and they have asked me, "Are you Kathy Pistoresi?" When I say "Yes," I either get a hug or a tear, or they say they have been praying for me for a long time. This always takes me by surprise! I ask how they knew about me. Most say through church, a prayer chain, or a friend. You see, God's audience is wide and deep!

Authoring this book has never been on my 'to-do list'; however, since 2012, I have shared my story time after time. Every time I speak, someone asks, "Are you going to write a book?" My family and friends often ask me, "Are you still writing a book?"

I began writing and journaling in 2012 about my feelings, my heartache, my joys, my losses. This led me to start asking questions about my hospital stay. Even though it was very painful to find out all the details, I wrote as Ken and others shared. Each year, I wrote pieces of my story.

In 2016, my husband and I were attending a business conference in Dallas, Texas. Howard Partridge has a multimillion-dollar carpet cleaning enterprise and helps other companies grow and market their business. We met Michelle Prince, who emcees Howard's conferences. She is a published author, has a publishing company, and was selling her book at this conference. I introduced myself, and by the time we finished our conversation, I had bought her book and signed up for her four-day conference, "Book Bound"!

I loved it! I met so many other "wannabe authors" and decided I would try to draft this book. But life got in the way. Drugs got in the way! Two years later, I went to Captiva Island, Florida, to attend my second Book Bound conference. Captiva Island is the most beautiful island I have ever visited. I mapped my book out again and shared my story with everyone. I met writers and authors with whom I stayed in touch today. I have watched them write and publish their books. I came home and started writing and adding to my manuscript, again!

Since then, I have had thousands of excuses for why I have not finished my book: my busy life, drugs, spinal fusion (surgery), money, pain, time, eye surgeries, (cataracts removed) and "I-Am-Not-a-Writer Syndrome," got in the way.

In December of 2021, after Covid racked our country and everyone had been feeling hopeless for almost two years, I decided to pray more about what God wanted me to do with my book. "Is this the right time, Lord, to finish and bring hope?" I asked.

In January of 2022, He answered my prayers! I was standing in the checkout line at Vons, and a woman I had never met before was in front of me. She turned and asked, "Are you Kathy Pistoresi?" I said, "Yes." "Have you written your book yet?" she said. "I'm in the process." "Your story needs to be told; it will give hope to many," she said. Wow, I know the Lord works in mysterious ways, but how did she know my name? One week later, the same thing happened in another store!

Since then, I have woken up every morning wanting to write and finish this book. On February 2, 2022, the tenth anniversary of me entering the hospital, I woke up thanking God for the last ten years. He said to me, "It's time to finish your book." I spent three weeks in Pismo Beach, California, house- and dog-sitting for a client. My time was spent writing, interviewing publishers, and walking and talking to God on the beach. We chose Michelle as our publisher.

I hope by now you have learned "Sickness is NOT my story." My story is all about God's mighty power and how He uses it through family, friends, and community. He gave me this story and this opportunity to tell you what is possible when you have faith bigger than your fears.

Prior to getting sick, I thought I was doing what God wanted me to do. I was fit and healthy and served my clients well. I felt strong in my faith. So, when I collapsed with asthma and was set aside to suffer, when I was consumed with pain, and when my life stopped, I was no longer of any use. I was no longer accomplishing anything. That is when Jesus said, "This is not about you." He taught me to be patient and submissive, to be still and listen, and from there, greater blessings would come through my suffering than when I thought I was doing my greatest work. As Max Lucado said, "Your pain has a purpose. Your problems, struggles, heartaches, and hassles cooperate toward one end – The Glory of God."

My prayer for you.... go out and find a church or community group of strong, God-fearing believers you can do life with. You will find that we are all broken people wanting to learn more about Jesus. Plus, a group like this prays together and stays together! You will receive love beyond your own understanding as you share your heart with others. You will be emotionally, spiritually, and physically supported through all the difficulties of life. Your faith will grow, and your life will be changed forever!

I never thought I would be the one God chose for this story. As I look back over the last eleven years, I am grateful for the journey, the pain, the suffering, the compassion, the love He sent my way. If you have ever thought you might be selected to struggle for God's glory, start preparing now. Fill your heart and soul with Scripture and the knowledge of who He really is.

My hope for you is when life happens and you need help, you will ask for it, pray for it, then trust the Lord to carry you the rest of the way home.

> *"Taste and see that the Lord is good; blessed is the one who takes refuge in him."*
> *(Psalm 34:8, NIV)*

www.ingramcontent.com/pod-product-compliance
Lightning Source LLC
Chambersburg PA
CBHW032130090426
42743CB00007B/548